MINDFUL MOMENTS

51 Inspirational Quotes, Real-Life Stories & Practices to Guide Your Path to Mindfulness, Well-being and Balance

Vishal Anand

Copyright © 2024 Vishal Anand

All rights reserved. No part of this publication may be reproduced, distributed or transmitted in any form or by any means, including photocopying, recording, or other electronic or mechanical methods, without the prior written permission of the author, except for brief quotations used in reviews.

For permissions, please contact the author at:
https://linktr.ee/vishhanand

CONTENTS

Title Page
Copyright
Introduction: Welcome to Your Journey of Mindful Moments　　1
Chapter 1: Awakening to the Present　　6
Chapter 2: Finding Inner Peace　　8
Chapter 3: Embracing Change　　10
Chapter 4: Cultivating Gratitude　　12
Chapter 5: Building Resilience　　14
Chapter 6: Nurturing Compassion　　16
Chapter 7: Harnessing Mindful Breathing　　18
Chapter 8: Letting Go of Attachments　　20
Chapter 9: Discovering Self-Acceptance　　22
Chapter 10: Creating Balance in Life　　24
Chapter 11: Understanding Emotional Intelligence　　26
Chapter 12: Developing Patience　　29
Chapter 13: The Power of Positive Thinking　　31
Chapter 14: Enhancing Self-Awareness　　33
Chapter 15: Fostering Mindful Relationships　　35

Chapter 16: Embracing Simplicity	37
Chapter 17: Living with Intention	39
Chapter 18: Transforming Stress into Strength	41
Chapter 19: Cultivating Forgiveness	43
Chapter 20: The Art of Letting Be	45
Chapter 21: Finding Purpose and Meaning	47
Chapter 22: Mindful Eating and Living	49
Chapter 23: Walking the Path of Mindfulness	51
Chapter 24: Sustaining Joy Through Mindfulness	53
Chapter 25: Harnessing the Power of Now	55
Chapter 26: Developing Mental Clarity	57
Chapter 27: Empowering Self-Discipline	59
Chapter 28: Embracing Silence and Stillness	61
Chapter 29: Living Authentically	63
Chapter 30: Mindful Leadership and Influence	65
Chapter 31: The Beauty of Mindful Living	68
Chapter 32: Cultivating a Growth Mindset	70
Chapter 33: Balancing Mind, Body, and Spirit	72
Chapter 34: Embracing Vulnerability	74
Chapter 35: The Journey to Self-Compassion	76
Chapter 36: Mindfulness in Everyday Actions	78
Chapter 37: Overcoming Fear with Mindfulness	80
Chapter 38: The Essence of Mindful Creativity	82
Chapter 39: Savoring the Present Moment	84
Chapter 40: Building a Mindful Routine	86
Chapter 41: Mindful Communication	88

Chapter 42: Discovering Inner Strength	90
Chapter 43: Nurturing Inner Joy	92
Chapter 44: Mindfulness and Emotional Healing	94
Chapter 45: Creating a Mindful Workspace	96
Chapter 46: Mindful Parenting and Family Life	99
Chapter 47: Connecting with Nature Mindfully	102
Chapter 48: Mindful Financial Well-being	104
Chapter 49: The Spirit of Mindfulness in Community	106
Chapter 50: Transcending Boundaries with Mindfulness	109
Chapter 51: self-compassion: turning kindness inward through mindfulness	111
Conclusion: Embracing Your Mindful Journey	115

INTRODUCTION: WELCOME TO YOUR JOURNEY OF MINDFUL MOMENTS

Welcome to "Mindful Moments: 51 Inspirational Quotes, Real-Life Stories & Practices to Guide Your Path to Mindfulness, Well-being and Balance." Whether you've picked up this book seeking solace, inspiration, or a fresh perspective, you've embarked on a transformative journey toward greater mindfulness and well-being. In the hustle and bustle of daily life, finding moments of peace and balance can feel elusive. This book is your companion, offering gentle guidance and profound insights to help you navigate the complexities of modern living with grace and presence.

Discover the Power of Mindfulness

Mindfulness is more than a buzzword; it's a way of being that invites us to fully engage with the present moment. It teaches us to observe our thoughts and feelings without judgment, fostering a deeper connection with ourselves and the world around us. Through mindfulness, we can cultivate resilience, reduce stress, and enhance our overall quality of life.

A Unique Structure for Your Unique Journey

Every chapter in this book is meticulously crafted to provide you with a meaningful and actionable experience. Each one follows a consistent structure, ensuring that you can seamlessly integrate these practices into your daily routine:

1. **Quotation:** Each chapter begins with a powerful quote that sets the tone and theme, offering wisdom from thought leaders, philosophers, and visionaries.
2. **Impactful Section Title:** A creative and evocative heading that captures the essence of the quote's message, drawing you deeper into the topic.
3. **Character Story:** A relatable narrative showcasing real-life experiences of individuals like us who embody the discussed principles, demonstrating how mindfulness has transformed their lives.
4. **Five-Step Implementation Plan:** Practical, easy-to-follow steps that guide you in applying the chapter's wisdom to your own life, making mindfulness accessible and actionable.
5. **Summary:** A concise recap that reinforces the key takeaways, encouraging you to reflect and implement what you've learned.

Your Path, Your Pace

One of the beautiful aspects of "Mindful Moments" is its flexibility. You're not required to read the chapters in any specific order. Whether you're seeking immediate relief from stress, looking to cultivate gratitude, or aiming to enhance your emotional intelligence, you can dive into any chapter that resonates with your current needs. Each chapter stands alone, offering valuable insights and practical steps that you can apply wherever you are in your mindfulness journey.

Creating Hope and Inspiring Change

This book is designed to evoke feelings of hope and inspiration. Life is filled with ups and downs, and sometimes we need a little extra encouragement to keep moving forward. "Mindful Moments" provides you with the tools to embrace each moment with intention, transforming challenges into opportunities for growth and joy. As you progress through the chapters, you'll discover how mindfulness can lead to profound personal transformation, helping you build a life that is not only balanced but also deeply fulfilling.

A Journey of Self-Discovery and Growth

Embarking on this journey means committing to your own well-being and personal growth. You'll explore various facets of mindfulness, from developing self-compassion and emotional resilience to fostering meaningful relationships and achieving work-life balance. Each chapter is a stepping stone, guiding you toward a more mindful, balanced, and joyful existence.

What to Expect

- **Inspirational Quotes:** Thought-provoking quotes that inspire and set the foundation for each chapter's theme.
- **Relatable Stories:** Engaging narratives that illustrate the practical application of mindfulness in everyday life.
- **Actionable Steps:** Clear, concise steps that empower you to implement mindfulness practices immediately.
- **Flexible Reading:** The ability to read chapters in any order, allowing you to focus on what matters most to you right now.

Embrace the Journey Ahead

As you turn the pages of "Mindful Moments," remember that each moment is an opportunity to cultivate mindfulness and enhance your well-being. Allow yourself to be present, embrace the wisdom shared within these chapters, and take actionable steps toward a more balanced and fulfilling life. This book is not just a collection of words; it's a roadmap to personal transformation and a testament to the incredible power of mindfulness.

Thank you for choosing **"Mindful Moments."** May this book inspire you, uplift you, and guide you toward a life filled with peace, balance, and profound well-being. Here's to your journey—may it be mindful, meaningful, and beautifully transformative.

With heartfelt gratitude and best wishes,

Vishal Anand

CHAPTER 1: AWAKENING TO THE PRESENT

"The present moment is filled with joy and happiness. If you are attentive, you will see it."
— Thich Nhat Hanh

Unlocking Presence

Thich Nhat Hanh encourages us to find joy in the here and now. By paying attention to the present, we can leave behind past worries and future anxieties, discovering true happiness in each moment.

Ella's Morning Routine

Ella, a 29-year-old marketing manager, often found herself rushing through mornings, barely having time for breakfast before heading to work. She felt stressed and disconnected from her day. Inspired by Thich Nhat Hanh's quote, Ella decided to wake up ten minutes earlier each morning to savor her coffee and practice mindful breathing. Over time, she noticed a significant decrease in her stress levels and began to enjoy her mornings more fully.

5 Steps to Embrace the Present

1. **Wake Up Earlier:** Allocate an extra ten minutes each morning to start your day calmly.
2. **Create a Peaceful Space:** Choose a quiet spot where you can enjoy your morning beverage without distractions.
3. **Practice Deep Breathing:** Spend a few minutes focusing on your breath to center your mind.
4. **Savor Your Breakfast:** Eat slowly and mindfully, appreciating each bite.
5. **Set Positive Intentions:** Reflect on one positive thing you want to achieve today.

Takeaway: Start Your Day with Presence

By incorporating these five steps, Ella transformed her hectic mornings into a peaceful and joyful start to her day. Embracing the present moment can help you find happiness in every part of your routine.

CHAPTER 2: FINDING INNER PEACE

"Peace comes from within. Do not seek it without."
— Buddha

Finding Serenity Within

Buddha reminds us that true peace is an internal state. Instead of looking for peace in external circumstances, we can cultivate it within ourselves through self-awareness and introspection.

Liam's Path to Tranquility

Liam, a 45-year-old entrepreneur, was constantly stressed by his demanding job and personal responsibilities. Determined to find peace, he began a nightly routine of meditation and journaling. This practice helped Liam calm his mind, improve his relationships, and gain a clearer perspective on his life's priorities.

5 Steps to Cultivate Inner Peace

1. **Set a Daily Meditation Time:** Dedicate 10 minutes each evening to meditate.
2. **Find a Quiet Space:** Choose a comfortable and silent place for your practice.
3. **Focus on Your Breath:** Use deep breathing to calm your mind and body.
4. **Journal Your Thoughts:** Write down your feelings and reflections to gain clarity.
5. **Practice Acceptance:** Acknowledge your emotions without judgment, fostering self-compassion.

Takeaway: Peace Begins Within

Through these five steps, Liam discovered that inner peace is achievable by looking inward. Cultivating serenity within yourself can lead to lasting tranquility and resilience.

CHAPTER 3: EMBRACING CHANGE

"Change is the only constant in life."
— Heraclitus

Adapting to Life's Flow

Heraclitus emphasizes that change is inevitable. Embracing change rather than resisting it allows us to grow and thrive amidst life's uncertainties.

Maya's Transformation Through Change

Maya, a 28-year-old teacher, faced sudden changes when her school implemented a new curriculum. Initially overwhelmed, Maya decided to view the change as an opportunity for growth. She attended professional development workshops, collaborated with her colleagues, and gradually adapted to the new system. Maya not only excelled in her role but also discovered a passion for innovative teaching methods.

5 Steps to Embrace Change

1. **Acknowledge the Change:** Accept that change is a natural part of life.
2. **Stay Open-Minded:** Be willing to explore new opportunities and perspectives.
3. **Develop Flexibility:** Adapt your plans and expectations as needed.
4. **Seek Support:** Connect with friends, family, or mentors during transitions.
5. **Reflect and Learn:** Assess the changes and identify lessons learned for future growth.

Takeaway: Grow with Change

By following these five steps, Maya turned her initial resistance into a journey of personal and professional growth. Embracing change empowers you to navigate life's transitions with confidence and grace.

CHAPTER 4: CULTIVATING GRATITUDE

"Gratitude turns what we have into enough."
— Aesop

Transforming Abundance

Aesop highlights the power of gratitude in shifting our perspective from scarcity to abundance. By appreciating what we have, we cultivate contentment and reduce feelings of wanting more.

Ethan's Gratitude Practice

Ethan, a 40-year-old software engineer, often felt discontent despite his successful career and supportive family. Inspired by Aesop's wisdom, he started writing down three things he was grateful for each evening. This simple practice shifted Ethan's focus from what he lacked to what he cherished, enhancing his overall happiness and satisfaction.

5 Steps to Cultivate Gratitude

1. **Choose Your Medium:** Select a journal or digital app to record your gratitudes.
2. **Set a Routine:** Dedicate time each day, preferably in the evening, to reflect on your blessings.
3. **Be Specific:** Identify particular moments, people, or things you appreciate.
4. **Reflect on Impact:** Consider how each item positively influences your life.
5. **Share Your Gratitude:** Express your thankfulness to others to deepen your connections.

Takeaway: Appreciate Abundance

Through these five steps, Ethan transformed his outlook, finding fulfillment in everyday moments. Cultivating gratitude can help you recognize and cherish the abundance in your life.

CHAPTER 5: BUILDING RESILIENCE

"The human capacity for burden is like bamboo—far more flexible than you'd ever believe at first glance."
— Jodi Picoult

Strength in Flexibility

Jodi Picoult uses the metaphor of bamboo to illustrate human resilience. Like bamboo, we can bend without breaking, adapting to challenges and bouncing back stronger from adversity.

Olivia's Resilient Spirit

Olivia, a 50-year-old nurse, faced burnout after years of intense work during the pandemic. Determined to reclaim her well-being, she implemented a resilience-building routine that included regular exercise, mindfulness meditation, and seeking support from peers. Over time, Olivia regained her strength, found renewed passion in her work, and became a pillar of support for her colleagues.

5 Steps to Build Resilience

1. **Acknowledge Your Feelings:** Allow yourself to experience and express your emotions.
2. **Seek Support:** Connect with friends, family, or professional counselors to share your struggles.
3. **Set Realistic Goals:** Break down challenges into manageable tasks to maintain progress.
4. **Maintain a Positive Outlook:** Focus on potential solutions and what you can control.
5. **Prioritize Self-Care:** Engage in activities that promote physical and mental well-being, such as exercise, hobbies, and adequate rest.

Takeaway: Flex Your Resilience

By following these five steps, Olivia turned her burnout into a journey of personal strength and professional rejuvenation. Building resilience empowers you to navigate life's challenges with grace and determination.

CHAPTER 6: NURTURING COMPASSION

"Compassion and tolerance are not a sign of weakness, but a sign of strength."
— Dalai Lama

Embracing Kindness

Dalai Lama teaches that compassion and tolerance are powerful strengths. By nurturing compassion, we build stronger, more empathetic connections with others and ourselves.

Tara's Compassionate Heart

Tara, a 53-year-old social worker, often felt overwhelmed by the emotional demands of her job. She decided to practice compassion towards herself and her clients by taking short breaks, practicing active listening, and showing kindness in small ways. This shift not only improved her well-being but also deepened her relationships with those she helped.

5 Steps to Nurture Compassion

1. **Practice Self-Compassion:** Be kind to yourself, especially during tough times.
2. **Active Listening:** Truly listen to others without interrupting or judging.
3. **Perform Acts of Kindness:** Engage in small acts of kindness daily, whether for yourself or others.
4. **Cultivate Empathy:** Try to understand things from another person's perspective.
5. **Reflect on Compassion:** Take time to think about how compassion has positively impacted your life and others'.

Takeaway: Strength Through Compassion

By embracing these five steps, Tara found that nurturing compassion not only enhanced her well-being but also strengthened her connections with others. Compassion is a true sign of strength that can transform lives.

CHAPTER 7: HARNESSING MINDFUL BREATHING

> *"Feelings come and go like clouds in a windy sky. Conscious breathing is my anchor."*
> — Thich Nhat Hanh

Anchoring with Breath

Thich Nhat Hanh illustrates how conscious breathing can serve as an anchor amidst the changing tides of our emotions. Mindful breathing helps us stay grounded and present.

Noah's Breathing Breaks

Noah, a 27-year-old graphic designer, struggled with

anxiety during tight project deadlines. He decided to incorporate mindful breathing breaks into his workday. By taking five minutes every few hours to focus on his breath, Noah found that his anxiety levels decreased, his focus improved, and he became more productive.

5 Steps to Harness Mindful Breathing

1. **Set Reminders:** Schedule short breaks throughout your day to practice breathing.
2. **Find a Comfortable Position:** Sit or stand in a relaxed posture.
3. **Focus on Your Breath:** Pay attention to each inhale and exhale without trying to change it.
4. **Count Your Breaths:** Count each breath cycle to help maintain focus.
5. **Return Gently:** If your mind wanders, gently bring your focus back to your breath without judgment.

Takeaway: Breathe Your Way to Calm

By integrating these five steps, Noah transformed his workday by reducing anxiety and enhancing focus. Harnessing mindful breathing can help you stay calm and centered, no matter the circumstances.

CHAPTER 8: LETTING GO OF ATTACHMENTS

"Attachment is the root of suffering."
— Buddha

Freeing Yourself from Clinging

Buddha teaches that attachment can lead to suffering. Letting go of what we cling to allows us to live more freely and peacefully.

Grace's Journey to Freedom

Grace, a 42-year-old teacher, found herself holding onto past relationships and unfulfilled dreams, which hindered her creativity and happiness. She decided to practice letting go by focusing on her present projects, seeking closure through reflection, and embracing new opportunities. This shift enabled Grace to rediscover her passion for art and find peace in her current life.

5 Steps to Let Go of Attachments

1. **Identify Attachments:** Recognize what you are holding onto that may be causing stress or unhappiness.
2. **Reflect on Impact:** Consider how these attachments affect your well-being and growth.
3. **Practice Acceptance:** Accept that some things are beyond your control and allow yourself to move forward.
4. **Focus on the Present:** Engage fully with the present moment instead of dwelling on the past or fearing the future.
5. **Embrace Change:** Welcome new experiences and opportunities with an open heart.

Takeaway: Embrace Freedom

By following these five steps, Grace let go of her attachments, leading to greater creativity and happiness. Letting go frees you to live more fully and peacefully.

CHAPTER 9: DISCOVERING SELF-ACCEPTANCE

> "To be yourself in a world that is constantly trying to make you something else is the greatest accomplishment."
> — Ralph Waldo Emerson

Embracing Your True Self

Ralph Waldo Emerson celebrates the importance of being true to oneself amidst societal pressures. Self-acceptance is a profound achievement that leads to genuine happiness.

Miraya's Path to Self-Love

Miraya, a 25-year-old student, struggled with self-doubt and the pressure to meet others' expectations. She decided to practice self-acceptance by engaging in positive self-talk, setting personal boundaries, and embracing her unique qualities. Over time, Miraya gained confidence, felt more authentic, and enjoyed greater fulfillment in her personal and academic life.

5 Steps to Discover Self-Acceptance

1. **Practice Positive Self-Talk:** Replace negative thoughts with affirming statements about yourself.
2. **Set Personal Boundaries:** Define what is acceptable for you in relationships and interactions.
3. **Embrace Your Strengths:** Acknowledge and celebrate your unique talents and qualities.
4. **Forgive Yourself:** Let go of past mistakes and treat yourself with kindness.
5. **Stay True to Your Values:** Live in alignment with your core beliefs and principles.

Takeaway: Embrace Your Authenticity

Through these five steps, Miraya discovered the power of self-acceptance, leading to increased confidence and fulfillment. Embracing who you truly are is the key to lasting happiness.

CHAPTER 10: CREATING BALANCE IN LIFE

"Balance is not something you find, it's something you create."
— Jana Kingsford

Crafting Your Equilibrium

Jana Kingsford emphasizes that balance is an active process. By consciously creating balance in our lives, we can achieve harmony and well-being.

Aiden's Balanced Lifestyle

Aiden, a 32-year-old software developer, often felt overwhelmed juggling work, family, and personal interests. He decided to create a balanced lifestyle by scheduling dedicated time for each aspect of his life, prioritizing tasks, and setting aside time for relaxation and hobbies. This intentional approach helped Aiden feel more in control, reduce stress, and enjoy a more harmonious daily routine.

5 Steps to Create Balance in Life

1. **Prioritize Your Tasks:** Identify what's most important and focus on those tasks first.
2. **Schedule Your Time:** Allocate specific times for work, family, and personal activities.
3. **Set Boundaries:** Define clear limits to prevent overcommitting and ensure time for yourself.
4. **Incorporate Relaxation:** Include activities that help you unwind and recharge, such as reading or taking walks.
5. **Regularly Assess:** Periodically evaluate your schedule and make adjustments to maintain balance.

Takeaway: Build Your Harmony

By implementing these five steps, Aiden successfully created a balanced lifestyle, reducing his stress and enhancing his overall well-being. Creating balance is a proactive way to achieve harmony in all areas of your life.

CHAPTER 11: UNDERSTANDING EMOTIONAL INTELLIGENCE

> "Emotional intelligence is the ability to recognize and manage your own emotions, and those of the people around you."
> — Daniel Goleman

Navigating Emotions with Clarity

Daniel Goleman highlights the importance of emotional intelligence in fostering healthy relationships and personal growth. By understanding and managing our emotions, we can enhance our interactions and overall well-being.

Isabella's Emotional Journey

Isabella, a 30-year-old human resources manager, often struggled with workplace conflicts and felt overwhelmed by her own emotions. Determined to improve, she enrolled in an emotional intelligence workshop. Through learning to recognize her feelings and empathize with her colleagues, Isabella transformed her work environment. She became a more effective leader, fostering a supportive and collaborative team.

5 Steps to Enhance Emotional Intelligence

1. **Self-Awareness:** Take time each day to reflect on your emotions and what triggers them.
2. **Self-Regulation:** Practice techniques like deep breathing or meditation to manage your responses.
3. **Empathy:** Make an effort to understand and share the feelings of others.
4. **Social Skills:** Improve your communication and conflict-resolution abilities.
5. **Motivation:** Set personal goals that inspire and drive you forward.

Takeaway: Master Your Emotions

By following these five steps, Isabella not only improved her emotional intelligence but also created a more harmonious and productive workplace. Enhancing your emotional intelligence can lead to stronger relationships and a more fulfilling life.

CHAPTER 12: DEVELOPING PATIENCE

"Patience is not simply the ability to wait – it's how we behave while we're waiting."
— Joyce Meyer

Cultivating Calm Amidst Waiting

Joyce Meyer emphasizes that patience goes beyond waiting; it involves maintaining a positive and composed attitude during the process. Developing patience can reduce stress and improve our interactions with others.

Ethan's Patience Practice

Ethan, a 40-year-old software engineer, found himself easily frustrated by long wait times and demanding customers. To build his patience, he began practicing mindfulness during his breaks, focusing on his breath and maintaining a calm demeanor. Over time, Ethan noticed a significant improvement in his ability to handle stressful situations, leading to better customer interactions and personal satisfaction.

5 Steps to Develop Patience

1. **Mindful Breathing:** Use deep breaths to stay calm during stressful moments.
2. **Set Realistic Expectations:** Understand that not everything happens instantly.
3. **Practice Delayed Gratification:** Choose to wait for rewards rather than seeking immediate satisfaction.
4. **Stay Present:** Focus on the current moment instead of worrying about the future.
5. **Reflect on Progress:** Acknowledge and celebrate small improvements in your patience.

Takeaway: Embrace Calmness

By implementing these five steps, Ethan transformed his impatience into calmness, enhancing both his professional and personal life. Developing patience allows you to navigate challenges with grace and maintain inner peace.

CHAPTER 13: THE POWER OF POSITIVE THINKING

> "Keep your face always toward the sunshine—and shadows will fall behind you."
> — Walt Whitman

Harnessing Optimism for a Brighter Future

Walt Whitman illustrates how maintaining a positive outlook can shift our perspective and attract positive outcomes. Positive thinking empowers us to overcome obstacles and embrace opportunities.

Lily's Optimistic Shift

Lily, a 24-year-old recent college graduate, felt discouraged after struggling to find a job in her field. Instead of succumbing to negativity, she chose to focus on her strengths and remain optimistic. Lily began visualizing her success, networking with confidence, and celebrating small victories. Her positive mindset attracted new opportunities, and soon, Lily secured a fulfilling position that aligned with her passions.

5 Steps to Cultivate Positive Thinking

1. **Affirmations:** Start your day with positive statements about yourself and your goals.
2. **Gratitude Journal:** Write down things you're thankful for each day to foster positivity.
3. **Surround Yourself with Positivity:** Engage with uplifting people and environments.
4. **Reframe Negative Thoughts:** Challenge and change negative perceptions into positive ones.
5. **Visualize Success:** Imagine achieving your goals to boost motivation and confidence.

Takeaway: Shine with Positivity

By adopting these five steps, Lily turned her job search into a journey of growth and optimism. Harnessing the power of positive thinking can transform your mindset and open doors to new possibilities.

CHAPTER 14: ENHANCING SELF-AWARENESS

"Self-awareness gives you the capacity to learn from your mistakes as well as your successes."
— Michelle Obama

Deepening Your Understanding of Self

Michelle Obama underscores the significance of self-awareness in personal development. By understanding our strengths, weaknesses, and emotions, we can make informed decisions and foster meaningful growth.

Marcus's Self-Discovery Journey

Marcus, a 35-year-old financial analyst, realized he was often reacting impulsively to stressful situations. Determined to improve, Marcus started practicing daily reflection, asking himself questions about his feelings and actions. Through this increased self-awareness, Marcus learned to manage his reactions better, leading to improved relationships and a more balanced professional life.

5 Steps to Enhance Self-Awareness

1. **Daily Reflection:** Spend a few minutes each day thinking about your actions and emotions.
2. **Seek Feedback:** Ask trusted friends or colleagues for honest insights about yourself.
3. **Mindfulness Practices:** Engage in activities like meditation to stay present and aware.
4. **Journaling:** Write down your thoughts and feelings to gain clarity.
5. **Set Personal Goals:** Define what you want to achieve and understand your motivations.

Takeaway: Know Yourself

By following these five steps, Marcus gained a deeper understanding of himself, leading to personal and professional improvements. Enhancing self-awareness is a crucial step towards achieving your full potential.

CHAPTER 15: FOSTERING MINDFUL RELATIONSHIPS

"The quality of your life is the quality of your relationships."
— Tony Robbins

Building Meaningful Connections

Tony Robbins highlights that the strength and quality of our relationships significantly impact our overall well-being. Mindful relationships are built on presence, empathy, and effective communication.

Sophie's Relationship Transformation

Sophie, a 32-year-old chef, noticed that her relationships with family and friends were strained due to her busy schedule and frequent distractions. Committed to improvement, Sophie started practicing mindful listening, giving her full attention during conversations, and expressing genuine empathy. These changes deepened her connections, making her relationships more fulfilling and supportive.

5 Steps to Foster Mindful Relationships

1. **Active Listening:** Pay full attention to others when they speak without interrupting.
2. **Express Empathy:** Show understanding and compassion towards others' feelings.
3. **Be Present:** Engage fully in interactions without distractions.
4. **Communicate Clearly:** Share your thoughts and feelings honestly and respectfully.
5. **Show Appreciation:** Regularly acknowledge and appreciate the people in your life.

Takeaway: Deepen Your Connections

By implementing these five steps, Sophie enriched her relationships, leading to greater happiness and support. Fostering mindful relationships enhances the quality of your life and those around you.

CHAPTER 16: EMBRACING SIMPLICITY

> "Simplicity is the ultimate sophistication."
> — Leonardo da Vinci

Finding Beauty in the Simple Things

Leonardo da Vinci celebrates the elegance of simplicity. By simplifying our lives, we can reduce stress, increase focus, and appreciate the fundamental joys of existence.

Noah's Minimalist Lifestyle

Noah, a 27-year-old graphic designer, felt overwhelmed by the clutter in his home and mind. Deciding to embrace simplicity, he decluttered his living space, minimized his possessions, and prioritized essential activities. This shift not only brought physical order but also mental clarity, allowing Noah to focus more on his creative projects and enjoy a more peaceful life.

5 Steps to Embrace Simplicity

1. **Declutter Your Space:** Remove unnecessary items to create a more organized environment.
2. **Prioritize Essentials:** Focus on what truly matters and let go of the rest.
3. **Simplify Your Schedule:** Reduce commitments and allocate time for relaxation.
4. **Practice Mindful Consumption:** Be intentional about what you buy and use.
5. **Focus on Quality Over Quantity:** Choose fewer, higher-quality items and experiences.

Takeaway: Live with Less

By adopting these five steps, Noah found that embracing simplicity led to a more organized, focused, and fulfilling life. Simplifying your life can help you appreciate the essential and eliminate unnecessary stress.

CHAPTER 17: LIVING WITH INTENTION

> "The things you do today can improve all your tomorrows."
> — Ralph Marston

Purposeful Living for a Meaningful Life

Ralph Marston emphasizes that living with intention involves making conscious choices that align with our values and goals. This purposeful approach leads to a more fulfilling and impactful life.

Mia's Purpose-Driven Choices

Mia, a 36-year-old graphic designer, felt her daily routine lacked meaning. She decided to live with intention by setting clear goals, aligning her work with her passions, and making mindful choices each day. This shift not only enhanced her productivity but also brought a sense of purpose and satisfaction to her life.

5 Steps to Live with Intention

1. **Define Your Values:** Identify what is most important to you.
2. **Set Clear Goals:** Establish specific, achievable objectives that align with your values.
3. **Make Conscious Choices:** Ensure your daily actions reflect your intentions.
4. **Prioritize Your Time:** Allocate time to activities that support your goals.
5. **Reflect Regularly:** Assess your progress and adjust your actions as needed.

Takeaway: Purposeful Progress

By following these five steps, Mia transformed her routine into a purpose-driven journey, leading to greater satisfaction and achievement. Living with intention empowers you to create a meaningful and impactful life.

CHAPTER 18: TRANSFORMING STRESS INTO STRENGTH

"It's not stress that kills us, it is our reaction to it."
— Hans Selye

Harnessing Stress for Personal Growth

Hans Selye teaches that our response to stress determines its impact on our lives. By transforming stress into strength, we can use challenging situations as opportunities for growth and resilience.

Ava's Strength Through Stress

Ava, a 40-year-old project manager, was constantly under pressure to meet tight deadlines. Instead of succumbing to stress, Ava began practicing stress-reduction techniques like exercise, meditation, and time management. This proactive approach not only reduced her stress levels but also enhanced her performance and resilience, allowing her to handle future challenges more effectively.

5 Steps to Transform Stress into Strength

1. **Identify Stressors:** Recognize what causes your stress.
2. **Develop Coping Strategies:** Implement techniques such as deep breathing, exercise, or meditation.
3. **Reframe Your Mindset:** View stress as a challenge rather than a threat.
4. **Build Resilience:** Strengthen your ability to recover from setbacks through positive habits.
5. **Seek Support:** Connect with others to share your experiences and gain perspective.

Takeaway: Grow Through Adversity

By adopting these five steps, Ava turned her stress into a source of strength and resilience. Transforming stress allows you to grow and thrive even in the face of challenges.

CHAPTER 19: CULTIVATING FORGIVENESS

"Forgiveness is not an occasional act, it is a constant attitude."
— Martin Luther King Jr.

The Healing Power of Forgiveness

Martin Luther King Jr. emphasizes that forgiveness is a continuous practice that fosters healing and peace. Cultivating forgiveness allows us to let go of resentment and move forward with our lives.

Lion's Path to Forgiveness

Lion, a 37-year-old lawyer, held onto resentment towards a former colleague who had wronged him. Determined to find peace, Lion decided to practice forgiveness by acknowledging his hurt, understanding the other person's perspective, and releasing his anger. This journey not only healed his emotional wounds but also improved his mental well-being and relationships.

5 Steps to Cultivate Forgiveness

1. **Acknowledge Your Feelings:** Recognize and accept the emotions you feel towards the situation.
2. **Understand the Other Perspective:** Try to see things from the other person's viewpoint.
3. **Let Go of Resentment:** Make a conscious decision to release negative feelings.
4. **Practice Empathy:** Cultivate compassion for yourself and others involved.
5. **Move Forward:** Focus on your growth and the positive aspects of your life.

Takeaway: Free Yourself Through Forgiveness

By following these five steps, Lion found that cultivating forgiveness brought him peace and emotional freedom. Embracing forgiveness allows you to heal and move forward with a lighter heart.

CHAPTER 20: THE ART OF LETTING BE

> "Sometimes letting things go is an act of far greater power than defending or hanging on."
> — Eckhart Tolle

Embracing Acceptance and Peace

Eckhart Tolle teaches that letting go can be more powerful than trying to control every situation. The art of letting be involves accepting things as they are and finding peace in that acceptance.

Emma's Practice of Letting Be

Emma, a 41-year-old writer, often felt anxious about the outcomes of her projects. Instead of constantly striving for perfection, she decided to practice letting be by accepting her efforts without judgment and focusing on the creative process. This shift reduced her anxiety, enhanced her creativity, and led to more fulfilling and successful projects.

5 Steps to Master the Art of Letting Be

1. **Accept What You Cannot Change:** Acknowledge situations beyond your control and let go of the need to change them.
2. **Release Attachment to Outcomes:** Focus on the process rather than obsessing over results.
3. **Embrace the Present:** Stay engaged with the current moment without dwelling on the past or future.
4. **Practice Mindfulness:** Use mindfulness techniques to stay grounded and calm.
5. **Trust the Process:** Have faith that things will unfold as they should without forcing or resisting.

Takeaway: Find Peace in Acceptance

By implementing these five steps, Emma learned to let go of her anxieties and embrace the flow of life. Mastering the art of letting be allows you to live more peacefully and authentically.

CHAPTER 21: FINDING PURPOSE AND MEANING

"The two most important days in your life are the day you are born and the day you find out why."
— Mark Twain

Discovering Your Why

Mark Twain emphasizes the significance of finding one's purpose in life. Understanding our "why" provides direction, motivation, and a sense of fulfillment, guiding us through both joyous and challenging times.

Ava's Quest for Meaning

Ava, a 40-year-old project manager, felt unfulfilled despite her successful career. She often wondered if there was more to life than her daily routine. Determined to find her purpose, Ava began volunteering at a local community center, exploring different interests and passions. Through these experiences, she discovered her love for teaching and mentoring young artists. Ava transitioned into a role that not only utilized her skills but also provided her with a deep sense of meaning and satisfaction.

5 Steps to Find Your Purpose and Meaning

1. **Reflect on Your Passions:** Identify activities and subjects that genuinely excite and interest you.
2. **Assess Your Strengths:** Determine what you're good at and how you can leverage these skills.
3. **Set Meaningful Goals:** Define clear and achievable objectives that align with your passions and strengths.
4. **Seek New Experiences:** Explore different activities, volunteer opportunities, or hobbies to discover what resonates with you.
5. **Connect with Others:** Engage with mentors, friends, or communities that share your interests and can provide guidance.

Takeaway: Live with Purpose

By following these five steps, Ava transformed her career and found profound satisfaction in her work. Finding your purpose brings clarity and direction, enabling you to lead a more meaningful and fulfilling life.

CHAPTER 22: MINDFUL EATING AND LIVING

"Let food be thy medicine and medicine be thy food."
— Hippocrates

Nourishing Body and Mind

Hippocrates highlights the connection between what we eat and our overall health. Mindful eating involves being present during meals, making conscious food choices, and appreciating the nourishment our bodies receive.

Deepak's Journey to Mindful Eating

Deepak, a 51-year-old technology executive , often ate on the go due to his busy schedule, leading to unhealthy eating habits and low energy levels. He decided to practice mindful eating by setting aside time for meals, savoring each bite, and choosing nutritious foods. This change not only improved his physical health but also enhanced his mental clarity and emotional well-being, allowing him to be more present both at work and home.

5 Steps to Practice Mindful Eating and Living

1. **Create a Calm Eating Environment:** Eat without distractions like TV or smartphones to fully focus on your meal.
2. **Savor Each Bite:** Chew slowly and enjoy the flavors, textures, and aromas of your food.
3. **Listen to Your Body:** Pay attention to hunger and fullness cues to avoid overeating.
4. **Choose Nutrient-Rich Foods:** Opt for whole, unprocessed foods that nourish your body and mind.
5. **Express Gratitude:** Take a moment to appreciate the effort and resources that went into your meal.

Takeaway: Eat with Awareness

By adopting these five steps, Deepak transformed his eating habits and overall lifestyle. Mindful eating fosters a healthier relationship with food, enhancing both physical and mental well-being.

CHAPTER 23: WALKING THE PATH OF MINDFULNESS

"The journey of a thousand miles begins with one step."
— Lao Tzu

Starting Your Mindfulness Journey

Lao Tzu reminds us that every significant journey begins with a single step. Walking the path of mindfulness involves continuous effort and commitment to living consciously and peacefully.

Ethan's Mindful Journey

Ethan, a 40-year-old software engineer, felt overwhelmed by the demands of his career and personal life. He decided to embark on a mindfulness journey by incorporating daily meditation, practicing gratitude, and being more present in his interactions. Over time, Ethan noticed reduced stress, improved focus, and deeper connections with loved ones, making his daily life more harmonious and fulfilling.

5 Steps to Walk the Path of Mindfulness

1. **Begin with Small Steps:** Start with a few minutes of mindfulness practice each day and gradually increase the time.
2. **Incorporate Mindfulness into Daily Activities:** Practice being present during routine tasks like washing dishes or walking.
3. **Develop a Meditation Routine:** Set aside a specific time each day for meditation to cultivate inner peace.
4. **Practice Gratitude:** Regularly acknowledge and appreciate the positive aspects of your life.
5. **Stay Consistent:** Make mindfulness a regular part of your life to experience long-term benefits.

Takeaway: Take the First Step

By following these five steps, Ethan successfully walked the path of mindfulness, leading to a more balanced and peaceful life. Starting your mindfulness journey can transform your perspective and enhance your overall well-being.

CHAPTER 24: SUSTAINING JOY THROUGH MINDFULNESS

"Joy is not in things; it is in us."
— Richard Wagner

Finding Joy Within

Richard Wagner emphasizes that true joy comes from within, not from external possessions or circumstances. Sustaining joy through mindfulness involves nurturing positive emotions and appreciating the present moment.

Sophia's Joyful Mindfulness Practice

Sophia, a 36-year-old social worker, often found herself bogged down by the stresses of her demanding job. Determined to find lasting joy, she began a daily mindfulness practice that included gratitude journaling, mindful breathing, and engaging in activities she loved. This approach helped Sophia maintain a positive outlook, even during challenging times, allowing her to experience sustained joy and fulfillment in her life.

5 Steps to Sustain Joy Through Mindfulness

1. **Practice Gratitude Daily:** Write down things you're thankful for each day to cultivate positive emotions.
2. **Engage in Activities You Love:** Make time for hobbies and interests that bring you happiness.
3. **Stay Present:** Focus on the current moment to fully experience and appreciate it.
4. **Cultivate Positive Relationships:** Surround yourself with supportive and uplifting people.
5. **Embrace Mindful Breathing:** Use mindful breathing techniques to center yourself and enhance your mood.

Takeaway: Cultivate Inner Joy

By implementing these five steps, Sophia was able to sustain joy through mindfulness, leading to a more positive and fulfilling life. Sustaining joy comes from nurturing your inner happiness and appreciating each moment.

CHAPTER 25: HARNESSING THE POWER OF NOW

"Realize deeply that the present moment is all you have."
— Eckhart Tolle

Living Fully in the Present

Eckhart Tolle underscores the importance of the present moment. Harnessing the power of now means fully engaging with the here and now, letting go of past regrets and future anxieties.

Daniel's Present-Focused Life

Daniel, a 36-year-old architect, often found himself dwelling on past mistakes and worrying about future projects. Inspired by Eckhart Tolle's teachings, Daniel began practicing present-focused techniques such as mindful walking and focusing on his breath. This shift allowed him to enjoy his work more, reduce stress, and build stronger relationships by being fully present with others.

5 Steps to Harness the Power of Now

1. **Focus on the Present:** Direct your attention to what you're doing right now, without distractions.
2. **Practice Mindful Breathing:** Use your breath as an anchor to stay grounded in the present moment.
3. **Let Go of the Past:** Release regrets and learn from past experiences without dwelling on them.
4. **Release Future Worries:** Trust that the future will unfold as it should, without overthinking it.
5. **Engage Fully:** Immerse yourself in your current activities and interactions to enhance your experience.

Takeaway: Embrace the Present

By adopting these five steps, Daniel transformed his life by fully embracing the present moment. Harnessing the power of now allows you to live more authentically and enjoy each moment to its fullest.

CHAPTER 26: DEVELOPING MENTAL CLARITY

"Clarity about your purpose leads to clarity in your mind."
— Steve Maraboli

Achieving a Clear Mind

Steve Maraboli highlights the link between purpose and mental clarity. Developing mental clarity involves organizing your thoughts, reducing distractions, and focusing on what truly matters.

Mia's Clear Mind Strategy

Mia, a 36-year-old graphic designer, struggled with creative blocks and scattered thoughts. Determined to enhance her mental clarity, Mia established a daily routine that included journaling, setting clear goals, and practicing mindfulness meditation. These practices helped Mia organize her thoughts, eliminate distractions, and foster a clear and focused mind, leading to increased productivity and creativity in her writing.

5 Steps to Develop Mental Clarity

1. **Set Clear Goals:** Define what you want to achieve to provide direction and focus.
2. **Practice Mindfulness Meditation:** Spend time each day meditating to clear your mind.
3. **Organize Your Environment:** Keep your workspace tidy to reduce mental clutter.
4. **Limit Distractions:** Identify and minimize sources of distraction in your daily life.
5. **Prioritize Tasks:** Focus on the most important tasks first to maintain clarity and efficiency.

Takeaway: Clear Your Mind

By implementing these five steps, Mia achieved greater mental clarity, enhancing her creativity and productivity. Developing mental clarity helps you stay focused and aligned with your goals, leading to a more purposeful life.

CHAPTER 27: EMPOWERING SELF-DISCIPLINE

"Discipline is the bridge between goals and accomplishment."
— Jim Rohn

Building Strong Habits

Jim Rohn emphasizes the role of discipline in achieving our goals. Empowering self-discipline involves developing consistent habits, staying committed, and overcoming obstacles to reach our desired outcomes.

Oliver's Discipline Transformation

Oliver, a 29-year-old entrepreneur, aspired to grow his small business but struggled with procrastination and inconsistency. To build self-discipline, Oliver created a structured daily schedule, set specific goals, and held himself accountable through regular progress reviews. This disciplined approach enabled Oliver to stay focused, overcome challenges, and successfully expand his business, achieving the accomplishments he had long desired.

5 Steps to Empower Self-Discipline

1. **Set Clear Goals:** Define specific and achievable objectives to guide your efforts.
2. **Create a Routine:** Establish a consistent daily schedule to build strong habits.
3. **Eliminate Temptations:** Remove distractions and triggers that hinder your progress.
4. **Stay Accountable:** Track your progress and hold yourself responsible for your actions.
5. **Reward Yourself:** Celebrate small victories to reinforce disciplined behavior.

Takeaway: Bridge to Success

By following these five steps, Oliver empowered himself with self-discipline, leading to the successful growth of his business. Empowering self-discipline is essential for turning your goals into tangible accomplishments.

CHAPTER 28: EMBRACING SILENCE AND STILLNESS

"Silence is a source of great strength."
— Lao Tzu

Finding Power in Stillness

Lao Tzu teaches that silence and stillness are powerful tools for inner strength and clarity. Embracing these states allows us to connect deeply with ourselves and find peace amidst chaos.

Grace's Quiet Strength

Grace, a 42-year-old teacher, felt constantly overwhelmed by the noise and demands of her daily life. She decided to incorporate moments of silence and stillness into her routine by practicing meditation, enjoying quiet walks in nature, and setting aside time for reflection. These practices helped Grace regain her inner strength, reduce stress, and enhance her ability to handle life's challenges with calm and clarity.

5 Steps to Embrace Silence and Stillness

1. **Schedule Quiet Time:** Allocate specific times each day for silence and stillness.
2. **Practice Meditation:** Use meditation techniques to cultivate inner peace and focus.
3. **Enjoy Nature:** Spend time in natural settings to experience tranquility and stillness.
4. **Limit Noise Exposure:** Reduce exposure to loud environments and unnecessary noise.
5. **Reflect Regularly:** Take moments to contemplate and connect with your inner self.

Takeaway: Strength in Stillness

By embracing silence and stillness, Grace found the inner strength to navigate her busy life with greater ease and peace. Embracing these moments allows you to recharge, find clarity, and build resilience.

CHAPTER 29: LIVING AUTHENTICALLY

> "To be yourself in a world that is constantly trying to make you something else is the greatest accomplishment."
> — Ralph Waldo Emerson

Being True to Yourself

Ralph Waldo Emerson celebrates the importance of authenticity. Living authentically means embracing who you are, aligning your actions with your true self, and resisting societal pressures to conform.

Ella's Authentic Life

Ella, a 29-year-old marketing manager, often felt pressured to follow trends rather than her own creative instincts. Determined to live authentically, Ella began designing clothes that reflected her personal style and values.

This shift not only brought her greater satisfaction and creativity but also attracted customers who appreciated her genuine approach, leading to a thriving and fulfilling business.

5 Steps to Live Authentically

1. **Know Yourself:** Spend time understanding your values, beliefs, and passions.
2. **Express Your True Self:** Let your actions and words reflect who you truly are.
3. **Set Boundaries:** Protect your authenticity by setting limits on what you will accept from others.
4. **Embrace Vulnerability:** Share your true feelings and experiences with others.
5. **Stay True to Your Values:** Make decisions that align with your core principles, even when it's challenging.

Takeaway: Be True to You

By following these five steps, Ella embraced her authenticity, leading to a more creative and fulfilling life. Living authentically allows you to express your true self and find genuine happiness and success.

CHAPTER 30: MINDFUL LEADERSHIP AND INFLUENCE

"Leadership is not about being in charge. It's about taking care of those in your charge."
— Simon Sinek

Leading with Mindfulness

Simon Sinek emphasizes that true leadership is about serving others and fostering their growth. Mindful leadership involves being present, empathetic, and intentional in guiding and supporting those you lead.

Varun's Mindful Leadership

Varun, a 45-year-old senior technology executive, noticed a decline in his team's morale and productivity due to over work. Determined to make a positive change, Varun adopted mindful leadership practices by actively listening to his team members, showing empathy, and encouraging open communication. This approach created a supportive and motivated team environment, leading to improved performance and job satisfaction among his team members.

5 Steps to Practice Mindful Leadership and Influence

1. **Listen Actively:** Pay full attention to your team members' ideas and concerns without interrupting.
2. **Show Empathy:** Understand and acknowledge the emotions and perspectives of others.
3. **Communicate Clearly:** Share your vision and expectations transparently and respectfully.
4. **Lead by Example:** Demonstrate the behaviors and values you expect from your team.
5. **Encourage Growth:** Support your team's professional and personal development through feedback and opportunities.

Takeaway: Lead with Presence

By implementing these five steps, Varun transformed his leadership style, fostering a motivated and cohesive team. Mindful leadership creates a positive and productive environment, enhancing both individual and collective success.

CHAPTER 31: THE BEAUTY OF MINDFUL LIVING

"The beauty of life is in small details, not in big events."
— Jim Jarmusch

Appreciating the Little Things

Jim Jarmusch reminds us that true beauty lies in the small, everyday moments. By practicing mindfulness, we can savor these details and enrich our lives with gratitude and joy.

Chetna's Appreciation Practice

Chetna, a 51-year-old operations manager, often overlooked the simple pleasures in her busy life, feeling constantly pressed for time. Determined to change, she started a daily gratitude journal, noting small moments of beauty like a blooming flower or a kind gesture from a colleague. This practice helped Chetna feel more connected to her surroundings, enhancing her overall happiness and sense of fulfillment.

5 Steps to Embrace Mindful Living

1. **Start a Gratitude Journal:** Write down three small things you're grateful for each day.
2. **Slow Down:** Take time to appreciate the details in your environment, such as the taste of your coffee or the sound of birds.
3. **Engage Your Senses:** Fully experience what you're doing by focusing on sight, sound, smell, taste, and touch.
4. **Practice Mindful Breathing:** Use breathing exercises to stay present and grounded in the moment.
5. **Celebrate Small Wins:** Acknowledge and celebrate minor achievements and joyful moments throughout your day.

Takeaway: Find Beauty in Every Moment

By following these five steps, Chetna transformed her perspective, finding beauty and joy in the simplest aspects of life. Embracing mindful living helps you appreciate the present and enhances your overall well-being.

CHAPTER 32: CULTIVATING A GROWTH MINDSET

"The only way to do great work is to love what you do."
— Steve Jobs

Embracing Continuous Growth

Steve Jobs emphasizes the importance of loving what you do to achieve greatness. Cultivating a growth mindset involves embracing challenges, learning from failures, and continuously seeking improvement.

Ethan's Growth Journey

Ethan, a 40-year-old software engineer, felt stuck in his routine job, fearing that he wasn't advancing in his career. Inspired by Steve Jobs' words, Ethan decided to adopt a growth mindset by taking online courses, seeking feedback, and embracing new projects. This proactive approach not only enhanced his skills but also reignited his passion for his work, leading to a promotion and greater job satisfaction.

5 Steps to Cultivate a Growth Mindset

1. **Embrace Challenges:** View challenges as opportunities to learn and grow rather than obstacles.
2. **Learn from Feedback:** Seek constructive criticism and use it to improve your skills and performance.
3. **Celebrate Effort:** Acknowledge the hard work and dedication you put into your endeavors.
4. **Persist Through Setbacks:** Stay committed to your goals even when faced with difficulties.
5. **Seek Continuous Learning:** Always look for ways to expand your knowledge and abilities through courses, books, or mentorship.

Takeaway: Grow with Passion

By implementing these five steps, Ethan transformed his career and found renewed passion in his work. Cultivating a growth mindset empowers you to achieve greatness by fostering a love for what you do and a commitment to continuous improvement.

CHAPTER 33: BALANCING MIND, BODY, AND SPIRIT

> "Take care of your body. It's the only place you have to live."
> — Jim Rohn

Achieving Holistic Harmony

Jim Rohn highlights the importance of caring for our physical selves as a foundation for overall well-being. Balancing mind, body, and spirit involves nurturing each aspect to achieve holistic harmony and health.

Korali's Holistic Balance

Korali, a 40-year-old yoga instructor, struggled to balance her demanding teaching schedule with personal well-being. She decided to integrate practices that nurtured her mind, body, and spirit by meditating daily, maintaining a regular exercise routine, and engaging in creative hobbies like painting. This balanced approach not only improved Korali's health but also enhanced her energy and enthusiasm for teaching.

5 Steps to Balance Mind, Body, and Spirit

1. **Establish a Routine:** Create a daily schedule that includes time for mental, physical, and spiritual activities.
2. **Practice Mindfulness:** Incorporate mindfulness techniques like meditation or deep breathing to calm the mind.
3. **Stay Active:** Engage in regular physical exercise that you enjoy, such as yoga, walking, or dancing.
4. **Nurture Your Spirit:** Participate in activities that inspire and uplift your spirit, like reading, journaling, or creative pursuits.
5. **Prioritize Self-Care:** Make self-care a priority by ensuring you get enough rest, nutrition, and relaxation.

Takeaway: Harmonize Your Life

By following these five steps, Korali achieved a balanced and harmonious life, enhancing her overall well-being. Balancing mind, body, and spirit leads to a more fulfilling and energized existence.

CHAPTER 34: EMBRACING VULNERABILITY

"Vulnerability sounds like truth and feels like courage. Truth and courage aren't always comfortable, but they're never weakness."
— Brené Brown

Finding Strength in Openness

Brené Brown teaches that embracing vulnerability is a sign of strength and authenticity. By being open and honest about our feelings and experiences, we foster deeper connections and personal growth.

Lily's Courageous Openness

Lily, a 52-year-old graphic designer, often kept her emotions hidden to appear strong at work. Inspired by

Brené Brown, Lily decided to embrace vulnerability by sharing her challenges and seeking support from her colleagues. This openness not only strengthened her relationships but also created a more supportive and collaborative work environment, leading to increased creativity and job satisfaction.

5 Steps to Embrace Vulnerability

1. **Acknowledge Your Feelings:** Recognize and accept your emotions without judgment.
2. **Share Your Story:** Open up about your experiences and feelings with trusted individuals.
3. **Seek Support:** Don't hesitate to ask for help when needed, fostering deeper connections.
4. **Practice Self-Compassion:** Be kind to yourself when you feel vulnerable, understanding that it's a natural part of being human.
5. **Take Small Risks:** Gradually expose yourself to vulnerability by taking small steps, such as expressing your opinions or sharing your goals.

Takeaway: Strength Through Openness

By embracing vulnerability, Lily built stronger, more authentic relationships and created a supportive work environment. Embracing vulnerability allows you to connect deeply with others and fosters personal strength and growth.

CHAPTER 35: THE JOURNEY TO SELF-COMPASSION

"You yourself, as much as anybody in the entire universe, deserve your love and affection."
— Buddha

Cultivating Kindness Toward Yourself

Buddha emphasizes the importance of self-compassion in nurturing our well-being. The journey to self-compassion involves treating ourselves with the same kindness and understanding we offer to others.

Sidney's Self-Love Path

Sidney, a 35-year-old teacher, often criticized herself for not meeting her own high expectations. Determined to foster self-compassion, Sidney started practicing daily affirmations, setting realistic goals, and allowing herself to rest without guilt. Over time, Sidney developed a kinder relationship with herself, leading to increased confidence, reduced stress, and a more positive outlook on life.

5 Steps to Journey to Self-Compassion

1. **Practice Self-Affirmations:** Use positive statements to reinforce your self-worth and abilities.
2. **Set Realistic Goals:** Define achievable objectives to avoid unnecessary self-criticism.
3. **Allow Yourself to Rest:** Take breaks and rest without feeling guilty or unproductive.
4. **Embrace Imperfections:** Accept that making mistakes is part of being human and a path to growth.
5. **Nurture Yourself:** Engage in activities that bring you joy and relaxation, prioritizing your well-being.

Takeaway: Love Yourself

By following these five steps, Sidney nurtured a compassionate and loving relationship with herself. The journey to self-compassion enhances your overall well-being and fosters a positive and resilient mindset.

CHAPTER 36: MINDFULNESS IN EVERYDAY ACTIONS

"The smallest step in the right direction can turn out to be the biggest step of your life."
— Naomi Judd

Integrating Mindfulness into Daily Life

Naomi Judd highlights the impact of small, mindful actions in creating meaningful change. Incorporating mindfulness into everyday activities fosters a deeper connection with the present and enhances our overall experience of life.

Oliver's Everyday Mindfulness

Oliver, a 29-year-old entrepreneur, felt disconnected from his daily routine, often moving through tasks on autopilot.

Inspired by Naomi Judd, Oliver decided to integrate mindfulness into his everyday actions by paying full attention to each task, whether it was preparing lessons, interacting with students, or enjoying his meals. This mindful approach made Oliver feel more engaged, present, and fulfilled in his daily life.

5 Steps to Practice Mindfulness in Everyday Actions

1. **Be Present:** Focus on the current task without letting your mind wander.
2. **Engage Your Senses:** Notice the sights, sounds, smells, tastes, and textures in each activity.
3. **Slow Down:** Take your time with tasks to fully experience them without rushing.
4. **Remove Distractions:** Minimize interruptions by putting away devices and focusing on the task at hand.
5. **Reflect on Your Actions:** Take a moment to appreciate and acknowledge the effort you put into each activity.

Takeaway: Live Fully Every Day

By adopting these five steps, Oliver transformed his daily routine into a series of mindful and fulfilling actions. Practicing mindfulness in everyday activities enriches your life, making each moment more meaningful and enjoyable.

CHAPTER 37: OVERCOMING FEAR WITH MINDFULNESS

"Do one thing every day that scares you."
— Eleanor Roosevelt

Facing Fears with Awareness

Eleanor Roosevelt encourages us to confront our fears head-on. Overcoming fear with mindfulness involves acknowledging our fears, understanding their origins, and taking conscious steps to address them.

Sophia's Fearless Steps

Sophia, a 29-year-old graphic designer, feared public speaking, which limited her professional opportunities. Determined to overcome this fear, Sophia began practicing mindfulness techniques like deep breathing and visualization before presentations. She also joined a local speaking club to gradually build her confidence. Through consistent practice and mindful awareness, Sophia became a confident and effective public speaker, opening doors to new career advancements.

5 Steps to Overcome Fear with Mindfulness

1. **Identify Your Fears:** Acknowledge what you're afraid of and understand its impact on your life.
2. **Practice Mindful Breathing:** Use deep breathing to calm your mind and reduce anxiety when facing fears.
3. **Visualize Success:** Imagine yourself successfully overcoming your fear to build confidence.
4. **Take Gradual Steps:** Confront your fear in small, manageable steps to build resilience.
5. **Reflect on Progress:** Acknowledge and celebrate your achievements in overcoming fear.

Takeaway: Conquer with Calmness

By implementing these five steps, Sophia overcame her fear of public speaking and expanded her professional horizons. Overcoming fear with mindfulness empowers you to face challenges with courage and clarity.

CHAPTER 38: THE ESSENCE OF MINDFUL CREATIVITY

"Creativity takes courage."
— Henri Matisse

Nurturing Creativity Through Mindfulness

Henri Matisse emphasizes that creativity requires bravery and presence. The essence of mindful creativity lies in being present, embracing inspiration, and allowing yourself to explore new ideas without judgment.

Amara's Creative Awakening

Amara, a 31-year-old writer, struggled with creative blocks and self-doubt. Inspired by Henri Matisse, Amara decided to incorporate mindfulness into her creative process by setting aside quiet time for brainstorming, practicing free writing without judgment, and engaging in mindful observation of her surroundings for inspiration. This mindful approach reignited her creativity, leading to a surge of innovative ideas and a more fulfilling writing experience.

5 Steps to Embrace Mindful Creativity

1. **Create a Peaceful Workspace:** Designate a calm and inspiring area for your creative activities.
2. **Set Aside Quiet Time:** Allocate specific times for uninterrupted creative thinking and exploration.
3. **Practice Free Writing or Drawing:** Allow your ideas to flow without self-censorship or judgment.
4. **Seek Inspiration Mindfully:** Observe your environment and let everyday moments inspire your creativity.
5. **Reflect on Your Process:** Regularly assess and appreciate your creative journey and progress.

Takeaway: Create with Presence

By adopting these five steps, Amara unlocked her creative potential and found joy in her writing process. The essence of mindful creativity lies in being present and embracing the flow of inspiration without fear or judgment.

CHAPTER 39: SAVORING THE PRESENT MOMENT

"Yesterday is history, tomorrow is a mystery, today is a gift of God, which is why we call it the present."
— Bil Keane

Cherishing Today's Gift

Bil Keane beautifully captures the importance of valuing the present moment. Savoring the present involves fully engaging with the current experience, appreciating its uniqueness, and finding joy in the now.

Payal's Present-Focused Life

Payal, a 40-year-old entrepreneur and procurement expert, often felt overwhelmed by the demands of her business and personal responsibilities. Determined to live more fully, Payal began practicing savoring the present by taking mindful breaks, appreciating small victories, and spending quality time with loved ones without distractions. This shift allowed Payal to enjoy the richness of each moment, enhancing her happiness and reducing stress.

5 Steps to Savor the Present Moment

1. **Practice Mindful Breathing:** Use deep breaths to anchor yourself in the present.
2. **Engage Fully:** Focus completely on the task or activity you're doing without multitasking.
3. **Appreciate Small Joys:** Notice and celebrate the little things that bring you happiness each day.
4. **Disconnect from Devices:** Limit screen time to stay present and engaged with your surroundings.
5. **Reflect on the Now:** Take a moment to acknowledge and appreciate the current moment's significance.

Takeaway: Treasure Today

By following these five steps, Payal learned to savor the present moment, leading to increased happiness and a more balanced life. Savoring the present helps you make the most of each day, fostering a deeper sense of fulfillment and peace.

CHAPTER 40: BUILDING A MINDFUL ROUTINE

"Routine, in an intelligent man, is a sign of ambition."
— W.H. Auden

Creating Structured Mindfulness Practices

W.H. Auden recognizes the importance of routine in achieving personal goals. Building a mindful routine involves integrating mindfulness practices into your daily schedule to create consistency and support your well-being.

Olivia's Structured Mindfulness

Olivia, a 29-year-old nurse, struggled to maintain mindfulness practices amidst her hectic schedule. To build a mindful routine, Olivia set specific times for meditation, mindful walking during breaks, and evening reflections. By consistently incorporating these practices into her day, Olivia experienced reduced stress, improved focus, and a greater sense of control over her well-being.

5 Steps to Build a Mindful Routine

1. **Set Specific Times:** Allocate fixed times each day for mindfulness activities like meditation or journaling.
2. **Start Small:** Begin with short sessions and gradually increase the duration as you become more comfortable.
3. **Create a Dedicated Space:** Designate a quiet area in your home where you can practice mindfulness without interruptions.
4. **Use Reminders:** Set alarms or use visual cues to remind yourself to engage in mindfulness practices.
5. **Be Consistent:** Stick to your routine even on busy days to build and maintain the habit.

Takeaway: Consistency Breeds Calm

By implementing these five steps, Olivia successfully built a mindful routine that enhanced her well-being and productivity. Building a mindful routine fosters consistency, making mindfulness an integral and sustaining part of your daily life.

CHAPTER 41: MINDFUL COMMUNICATION

"The most important thing in communication is hearing what isn't said."
— Peter Drucker

Connecting Beyond Words

Peter Drucker highlights that true communication goes beyond spoken words. Mindful communication involves active listening, empathy, and understanding the unspoken emotions and intentions behind words.

Emma's Communication Transformation

Emma, a 41-year-old writer, noticed frequent misunderstandings and conflicts within her team. Determined to improve, she adopted mindful communication practices by actively listening to her team members, paying attention to non-verbal cues, and responding with empathy. This approach fostered a more harmonious and productive work environment, enhancing team collaboration and satisfaction.

5 Steps to Practice Mindful Communication

1. **Active Listening:** Focus entirely on the speaker without interrupting or planning your response.
2. **Observe Non-Verbal Cues:** Pay attention to body language, facial expressions, and tone of voice.
3. **Respond with Empathy:** Acknowledge the speaker's feelings and perspectives before responding.
4. **Ask Clarifying Questions:** Ensure understanding by seeking clarification when needed.
5. **Reflect Before Speaking:** Take a moment to consider your words to communicate clearly and thoughtfully.

Takeaway: Speak with Presence

By implementing these five steps, Emma transformed her team's communication, leading to stronger relationships and improved collaboration. Mindful communication deepens connections and fosters a supportive environment.

CHAPTER 42: DISCOVERING INNER STRENGTH

"You never know how strong you are until being strong is your only choice."
— Bob Marley

Unleashing Your Resilience

Bob Marley emphasizes that true strength often emerges in the face of adversity. Discovering inner strength involves recognizing your resilience, embracing challenges, and believing in your ability to overcome obstacles.

Lucas's Resilient Journey

Lucas, a 40-year-old firefighter, faced a life-threatening injury that left him physically and emotionally scarred. Determined to recover, Lucas tapped into his inner strength by setting small, achievable goals, seeking support from loved ones, and maintaining a positive mindset. Through perseverance and resilience, Lucas not only regained his physical health but also discovered a newfound sense of purpose and inner fortitude.

5 Steps to Discover Inner Strength

1. **Set Small Goals:** Break down larger challenges into manageable tasks to build confidence.
2. **Seek Support:** Lean on friends, family, or professionals for encouragement and assistance.
3. **Maintain a Positive Mindset:** Focus on your strengths and past successes to boost resilience.
4. **Embrace Challenges:** View obstacles as opportunities to grow and learn.
5. **Practice Self-Care:** Take care of your physical and emotional well-being to sustain your strength.

Takeaway: Harness Your Resilience

By following these five steps, Lucas unlocked his inner strength, enabling him to overcome significant challenges. Discovering your inner strength empowers you to navigate life's toughest moments with courage and determination.

CHAPTER 43: NURTURING INNER JOY

"Joy is what happens to us when we allow ourselves to recognize how good things really are."
— Marsha Norman

Cultivating Lasting Happiness

Marsha Norman teaches that joy arises when we acknowledge and appreciate the goodness in our lives. Nurturing inner joy involves intentional practices that foster gratitude, positivity, and mindfulness.

Sophia's Joyful Practice

Sophia, a 36-year-old social worker, often felt overwhelmed by the emotional demands of her job. To nurture her inner joy, Sophia started incorporating daily gratitude exercises, engaging in activities that brought her happiness, and practicing mindfulness meditation. These practices helped Sophia maintain a positive outlook, reduce stress, and experience sustained joy despite her challenging work environment.

5 Steps to Nurture Inner Joy

1. **Daily Gratitude:** Write down three things you're grateful for each day to focus on the positive.
2. **Engage in Joyful Activities:** Dedicate time to hobbies and interests that bring you happiness.
3. **Practice Mindfulness:** Stay present and fully experience each moment without judgment.
4. **Surround Yourself with Positivity:** Connect with uplifting people and environments.
5. **Celebrate Small Wins:** Acknowledge and appreciate your achievements, no matter how small.

Takeaway: Embrace Lasting Joy

By implementing these five steps, Sophia was able to sustain her inner joy, enhancing her overall well-being and resilience. Nurturing inner joy allows you to find happiness in everyday moments and maintain a positive outlook.

CHAPTER 44: MINDFULNESS AND EMOTIONAL HEALING

> "Healing takes courage, and we all have courage, even if we have to dig a little to find it."
> — Tori Amos

Releasing Emotional Pain

Tori Amos emphasizes that emotional healing requires bravery and a willingness to confront and release past hurts. Mindfulness plays a crucial role in this process by helping us stay present and manage our emotions effectively.

Amara's Healing Journey

Amara, a 35-year-old therapist, carried the weight of

unresolved trauma from her past. Determined to heal, Amara began a mindfulness-based therapy regimen, which included meditation, journaling, and guided imagery. Through these practices, Amara was able to process her emotions, release lingering pain, and rebuild her emotional strength, leading to a more balanced and fulfilling life.

5 Steps to Mindful Emotional Healing

1. **Acknowledge Your Emotions:** Recognize and accept your feelings without judgment.
2. **Practice Mindful Breathing:** Use deep breathing to stay grounded during emotional moments.
3. **Engage in Reflective Journaling:** Write about your experiences and emotions to gain clarity.
4. **Seek Support:** Connect with a therapist or support group to navigate your healing process.
5. **Embrace Self-Compassion:** Treat yourself with kindness and understanding as you heal.

Takeaway: Heal with Mindfulness

By following these five steps, Amara facilitated her emotional healing, finding peace and resilience. Mindful emotional healing empowers you to release pain and embrace a healthier, more balanced emotional state.

CHAPTER 45: CREATING A MINDFUL WORKSPACE

"Your work is going to fill a large part of your life, and the only way to be truly satisfied is to do what you believe is great work."
— Steve Jobs

Optimizing Your Environment for Productivity

Steve Jobs underscores the importance of a fulfilling work environment. Creating a mindful workspace involves organizing your physical space, minimizing distractions, and fostering a positive and productive atmosphere.

Ethan's Productive Workspace

Ethan, a 40-year-old software engineer, struggled with productivity in his cluttered and chaotic home office. Determined to enhance his work environment, Ethan redesigned his workspace by decluttering, adding calming elements like plants and natural light, and establishing clear boundaries between work and personal life. This mindful approach led to increased focus, greater efficiency, and a more enjoyable work experience.

5 Steps to Create a Mindful Workspace

1. **Declutter Your Space:** Remove unnecessary items to create a clean and organized environment.
2. **Incorporate Calming Elements:** Add plants, natural light, and soothing colors to enhance your workspace's ambiance.
3. **Set Clear Boundaries:** Define specific areas for work and relaxation to maintain a healthy work-life balance.
4. **Minimize Distractions:** Limit noise and interruptions by using noise-canceling headphones or creating a quiet zone.
5. **Personalize Thoughtfully:** Add personal touches that inspire and motivate you without causing clutter.

Takeaway: Optimize for Productivity

By implementing these five steps, Ethan transformed his workspace into a mindful and productive environment.

Creating a mindful workspace enhances focus, reduces stress, and fosters a more satisfying work experience.

CHAPTER 46: MINDFUL PARENTING AND FAMILY LIFE

"Children are not things to be molded, but are people to be unfolded."
— Jess Lair

Fostering Mindful Connections with Your Family

Jess Lair emphasizes the importance of nurturing your children's growth through mindful parenting. Mindful parenting involves being present, understanding, and supportive, allowing children to develop naturally and confidently.

Grace's Mindful Parenting Approach

Grace, a 44-year-old mother of two, struggled to

balance discipline with understanding in her parenting. Determined to improve, Grace adopted mindful parenting techniques by actively listening to her children, setting consistent and fair boundaries, and spending quality time together without distractions. This mindful approach strengthened her relationships with her children, fostering trust, respect, and mutual understanding within her family.

5 Steps to Practice Mindful Parenting

1. **Be Present:** Give your full attention to your children during interactions.
2. **Listen Actively:** Understand your children's feelings and perspectives without immediate judgment.
3. **Set Consistent Boundaries:** Establish clear and fair rules to provide structure and security.
4. **Encourage Independence:** Allow your children to explore and develop their own interests and abilities.
5. **Show Empathy and Support:** Be compassionate and supportive, helping your children navigate their emotions and challenges.

Takeaway: Nurture with Mindfulness

By following these five steps, Grace enhanced her parenting style, creating a loving and supportive family environment. Mindful parenting fosters strong, healthy relationships and supports your children's emotional and personal

growth.
———————————————————————

CHAPTER 47: CONNECTING WITH NATURE MINDFULLY

"Look deep into nature, and then you will understand everything better."
— Albert Einstein

Finding Peace Through Nature

Albert Einstein highlights the profound lessons and peace that nature offers. Connecting with nature mindfully involves being present in natural settings, appreciating their beauty, and using them as a source of inspiration and healing.

Noah's Nature Connection

Noah, a 27-year-old graphic designer, felt disconnected and stressed from his urban lifestyle. Determined to find peace, Noah began spending time in nature, practicing mindful walking in parks, hiking, and observing wildlife. This mindful connection with nature helped Noah reduce stress, enhance his creativity, and gain a deeper appreciation for the natural world around him.

5 Steps to Connect with Nature Mindfully

1. **Spend Time Outdoors:** Make it a habit to spend regular time in natural settings like parks, forests, or beaches.
2. **Practice Mindful Walking:** Walk slowly and pay attention to the sights, sounds, and smells around you.
3. **Engage Your Senses:** Fully experience nature by noticing the details through your senses.
4. **Reflect and Meditate:** Use natural surroundings as a backdrop for reflection and meditation.
5. **Appreciate Nature's Beauty:** Take moments to admire and appreciate the beauty and complexity of the natural world.

Takeaway: Embrace Nature's Gifts

By implementing these five steps, Noah deepened his connection with nature, finding peace and inspiration in the natural world. Mindfully connecting with nature enhances your well-being and fosters a greater appreciation for the environment.

CHAPTER 48: MINDFUL FINANCIAL WELL-BEING

"Do not save what is left after spending, but spend what is left after saving."
— Warren Buffett

Managing Finances with Awareness

Warren Buffett emphasizes the importance of disciplined financial management. Mindful financial well-being involves being conscious of your spending habits, setting financial goals, and making informed decisions to secure your future.

Chetna's Financial Transformation

Chetna, a 51-year-old operations manager, struggled with debt and impulsive spending, especially on the latest trending clothes and accessories. She had enough clothes to last at least two years, with many still tagged in her closet. Determined to take control, Chetna adopted mindful financial habits by budgeting, saving, and tracking her expenses. This not only eliminated her debt but also gave her peace of mind and financial security. She became much calmer, no longer panicking over credit card statements, as she finally had control over her finances.

5 Steps to Achieve Mindful Financial Well-being

1. **Create a Budget:** Outline your income and expenses to understand your financial situation.
2. **Prioritize Savings:** Allocate a portion of your income to savings before spending on non-essentials.
3. **Track Your Spending:** Monitor your expenses regularly to identify and reduce unnecessary spending.
4. **Set Financial Goals:** Define short-term and long-term financial objectives to guide your saving and spending habits.
5. **Practice Mindful Spending:** Make intentional and informed decisions about where and how you spend your money.

Takeaway: Secure Your Future

By following these five steps, Chetna achieved financial stability and peace of mind. Mindful financial well-being empowers you to manage your finances effectively, ensuring a secure and fulfilling future.

CHAPTER 49: THE SPIRIT OF MINDFULNESS IN COMMUNITY

"Alone we can do so little; together we can do so much."
— Helen Keller

Building Mindful and Supportive Communities

Helen Keller underscores the power of community in achieving collective well-being. The spirit of mindfulness in community involves fostering connections, supporting one another, and creating a harmonious and inclusive environment.

Parmod's Community Engagement

Parmod, a 65-year-old retired senior government official, noticed a lack of community spirit in his neighborhood. Determined to make a positive impact, Parmod organized mindful community events such as neighborhood clean-ups, meditation sessions, and group walks in the park. These initiatives brought residents together, fostering a sense of belonging, cooperation, and mutual support, transforming his community into a more mindful and connected place.

5 Steps to Foster Mindfulness in Community

1. **Organize Community Events:** Host activities that promote mindfulness, such as yoga classes, meditation workshops, or nature walks.
2. **Encourage Open Communication:** Create spaces for residents to share ideas, concerns, and support each other.
3. **Promote Inclusivity:** Ensure that all community members feel welcome and valued, regardless of their background.
4. **Collaborate on Projects:** Work together on community projects that benefit everyone, fostering teamwork and cooperation.
5. **Celebrate Together:** Acknowledge and celebrate community achievements and milestones to build a positive and united environment.

Takeaway: Unite with Mindfulness

By implementing these five steps, Parmod revitalized his community, fostering a supportive and mindful environment. The spirit of mindfulness in community enhances collective well-being and strengthens social bonds.

CHAPTER 50: TRANSCENDING BOUNDARIES WITH MINDFULNESS

"The mind is everything. What you think you become."
— Buddha

Expanding Beyond Limits

Buddha teaches that our thoughts shape our reality. Transcending boundaries with mindfulness involves breaking through self-imposed limitations, embracing growth, and envisioning a limitless potential.

Ella's Boundless Growth

Ella, a 29-year-old marketing manager, felt confined by her self-doubt and limited beliefs about her abilities. Inspired by Buddha's wisdom, Ella began practicing mindfulness to observe and transform her thought patterns. She set ambitious goals, sought new challenges, and embraced opportunities for growth. This mindful approach allowed Ella to transcend her perceived boundaries, leading to significant professional advancements and personal fulfillment.

5 Steps to Transcend Boundaries with Mindfulness

1. **Identify Limiting Beliefs:** Recognize thoughts that hold you back from reaching your potential.
2. **Practice Mindful Awareness:** Observe your thoughts without judgment to understand their impact.
3. **Challenge Negative Thoughts:** Replace limiting beliefs with positive and empowering ones.
4. **Set Ambitious Goals:** Define clear and challenging objectives to push your boundaries.
5. **Embrace Continuous Learning:** Seek opportunities to grow and expand your skills and knowledge.

Takeaway: Expand Your Horizons

By following these five steps, Ella overcame her self-imposed limitations and achieved remarkable growth. Transcending boundaries with mindfulness empowers you to realize your full potential and embrace a life of limitless possibilities.

CHAPTER 51: SELF-COMPASSION: TURNING KINDNESS INWARD THROUGH MINDFULNESS

> "You yourself, as much as anybody in the entire universe, deserve your love and affection."
> — Buddha

Why Self-Compassion Matters

In a world that constantly pushes us to achieve more and be more, we often forget the most important person in our lives—ourselves. We're quick to offer kindness to others but can be harshly critical when it comes to our own mistakes and shortcomings. Self-compassion is the practice of extending the same kindness, understanding, and care to ourselves that we so easily give to others.

Through mindfulness, we learn to quiet the inner critic and embrace self-compassion, allowing ourselves to grow, heal, and thrive without judgment.

Nina's Journey to Self-Compassion

Nina, a 45-year-old teacher, had always been hard on herself. Despite being praised by her students and colleagues, she constantly felt like she wasn't doing enough. Every mistake she made, whether big or small, haunted her for days, feeding a relentless cycle of self-criticism. Eventually, the stress started to take a toll on her health and well-being.

One day, Nina stumbled upon a mindfulness practice focused on self-compassion. At first, it felt foreign to treat herself with kindness, but she was determined to break free from her critical thoughts. Through daily mindfulness meditations, Nina began to observe her negative self-talk without judgment and gradually replaced it with affirmations of love and care. She started treating herself as she would a close friend—understanding and accepting, even when things didn't go perfectly. Over time, Nina felt lighter, more energized, and less trapped by her inner critic.

Self-compassion didn't make Nina less driven; in fact, it empowered her to approach her life with more confidence, resilience, and joy.

5 Steps to Cultivate Self-Compassion with Mindfulness

1. **Notice Your Inner Critic:** Pay attention to the way you talk to yourself. Notice when self-critical thoughts

arise, but don't engage with them. Simply observe them as passing thoughts rather than facts.

2. **Practice Self-Soothing:** When you feel overwhelmed or down on yourself, place a hand on your heart or give yourself a comforting gesture. These small actions activate feelings of warmth and care toward yourself.

3. **Talk to Yourself Like a Friend:** Next time you make a mistake or feel inadequate, ask yourself: "What would I say to a close friend in this situation?" Practice offering the same kindness and understanding to yourself.

4. **Use Mindful Affirmations:** Incorporate affirmations like "I am enough," or "It's okay to make mistakes, I'm still learning." Repeat these during mindfulness practices to reinforce self-compassion.

5. **Accept Imperfection as Part of the Journey:** Mindfulness teaches us that life is imperfect and constantly changing. Embrace your flaws as part of your growth, and recognize that everyone makes mistakes—what matters is how you treat yourself in those moments.

Takeaway: Be Your Own Source of Compassion

Nina's story reminds us that the harshest critic often lives within, but mindfulness gives us the tools to change that. Self-compassion is not about becoming complacent or ignoring our responsibilities—it's about nurturing ourselves with kindness so that we can face life's challenges with strength and resilience. By turning compassion inward, we create space for healing, growth, and happiness.

CONCLUSION: EMBRACING YOUR MINDFUL JOURNEY

As you reach the end of **"Mindful Moments: 51 Inspirational Quotes, Real-Life Stories & Practices to Guide Your Path to Mindfulness, Well-being and Balance,"** take a moment to reflect on the transformative journey you've embarked upon. Each chapter has offered you a beacon of wisdom, a stepping stone towards greater mindfulness, and practical steps to integrate compassion and presence into every facet of your life.

Through the diverse and heartfelt stories of Ella, Liam, Grace, Lucas, and many others, you've witnessed the profound impact of mindfulness on personal growth, relationships, and overall well-being. These moments of insight and practice are not merely pages in a book; they are invitations to awaken your own mindful moments and cultivate a life of balance, joy, and resilience.

Remember:

- **Embrace the Present:** Each moment is a gift

waiting to be cherished.

- **Cultivate Inner Peace:** Find serenity within yourself, regardless of external circumstances.
- **Foster Compassion:** Extend kindness and understanding to yourself and others.
- **Nurture Your Growth:** Continuously seek personal and professional development.
- **Connect Deeply:** Build meaningful relationships through mindful communication and presence.
- **Celebrate Simplicity:** Appreciate the beauty in the small, everyday moments.
- **Live Authentically:** Stay true to who you are, embracing your unique journey.
- **Build Resilience:** Turn challenges into opportunities for strength and growth.
- **Find Joy:** Sustain happiness by recognizing and nurturing the good in your life.
- **Transcend Boundaries:** Push beyond your limits with a mindset of limitless potential.

As the author, I want to express my heartfelt gratitude to you for choosing this book as a companion on your path to mindfulness and well-being. Your commitment to personal growth and your willingness to embrace these practices inspire me deeply. May the wisdom and practices shared within these pages empower you to lead a life filled with compassion, presence, and enduring happiness.

Wishing you all the best on your mindful journey. May each moment bring you closer to the balanced and fulfilling life you deserve.

With gratitude and warm wishes,

Vishal Anand

Urgent Plea!

Thank you for reading my book. If this book has helped you in your journey toward mindfulness, here's how you can help spread the word and stay connected.

Leave a Review: Your feedback makes a huge difference in helping others discover this book. Whether you purchased it on Amazon, Apple Books, Google Play, or another platform, I would really appreciate it if you could take a moment to leave a review.

Stay Connected & Continue Your Transformation: This journey is just getting started. Visit www.TheVishalAnand.com for updates on upcoming books, courses, and epic tools to help you transform even more areas of your life!

Thank you so much for your support!

Vishal Anand